COVENANT · BIBLE · STUDIES

James
Faith in Action

David S. Young

faithQuest
the trade imprint of Brethren Press

Covenant Bible Study Series

James: Faith in Action

David S. Young

Unless otherwise noted, scripture quotations are from the New Revised Standard Version of the Bible, copyrighted 1989 by the National Council of Churches of Christ in the USA, Division of Education and Ministry.

Cover design by Jeane Healy
Cover Photograph by Marc Romanelli / The Image Bank

Library of Congress Catalog Card Number: 92-54258

Manufactured in the United States of America

Contents

Foreword

The Covenant Bible Study Series was first developed for a denominational program in the Church of the Brethren and the Christian Church (Disciples of Christ). This program, called People of the Covenant, was founded on the concept of relational Bible study and has been adopted by several other denominations and small groups who want to study the Bible in a community rather than alone.

Relational Bible study is marked by certain characteristics, some of which differ from other types of Bible study. For one, it is intended for small groups of people who can meet face-to-face on a regular basis and share frankly with an intimate group.

It is important to remember that relational Bible study is anchored in covenantal history. God covenanted with people in Old Testament history, established a new covenant in Jesus Christ, and covenants with the church today.

Relational Bible study takes seriously a corporate faith. As each person contributes to study, prayer, and work, the group becomes the real body of Christ. Each one's contribution is needed and important. "For just as the body is one and has many members, and all the members of the body, though many, are one body, so it is with Christ. . . . Now you are the body of Christ and individually members of it" (1 Cor. 12:12, 17).

Relational Bible study helps both individuals and the group to claim the promise of the Spirit and the working of the Spirit. As one person testified, "In our commitment to one another and in our sharing, something happened. . . . We were woven together in love by the master Weaver. It is something that can happen only when two or three or seven are gathered in God's name, and we know the promise of God's presence in our lives."

The symbol for these covenant Bible study groups is the burlap cross. The interwoven threads, the uniqueness of each strand, the unrefined fabric, and the rough texture characterize covenant groups. The people in the groups are unique but interrelated; they are imperfect and unpolished, but loving and supportive.

The shape that these divergent threads create is the cross, the symbol for all Christians of the resurrection and presence with us of Christ our Savior. Like the burlap cross, we are brought together, simple and ordinary, to be sent out again in all directions to be in the world.

For people who choose to use this study in a small group, the following guidelines will help create an atmosphere in which support will grow and faith will deepen.

1. As a small group of learners, we gather around God's word to discern its meaning for today.
2. The words, stories, and admonitions we find in scripture come alive for today, challenging and renewing us.
3. All people are learners and all are leaders.
4. Each person will contribute to the study, sharing the meaning found in the scripture and helping to bring meaning to others.
5. We recognize each other's vulnerability as we share out of our own experience, and in sharing we learn to trust others and to be trustworthy.

Additional suggestions for study and group-building are provided in the "Sharing and Prayer" section. They are intended for use in the hour preceding the Bible study to foster intimacy in the covenant group and relate personal sharing to the Bible study topic.

Welcome to this study. As you search the scriptures, may you also search yourself. May God's voice and guidance and the love and encouragement of brothers and sisters in Christ challenge you to live more fully the abundant life God promises.

Preface

Even as a child I saw that faith was more than deep belief. My mother, who saw to my religious education, and my grandmother, whom I could see from my crib as she prayed and worked, showed me that faith is a way of life. In our household there was no "double-mindedness," as James calls it, no allegiance to Christ on one hand and allegiance to the ways of this world on the other. My models for life put their faith into action.

One of the greatest challenges for the Christian in today's society is to know exactly how to live the Christian life. How do we choose the best option when there are so many choices and so many pressures under which to make them?

The Letter of James is a handbook to help Christians in a secular culture know how to respond in faith to very practical problems, problems that are as relevant today as they were for early Christians. "Count it all joy," James says. For in every age, faith matures and is strengthened by the tests and trials it encounters. Faith only grows by action.

For James, this is what faith is. Rather than a set of vague beliefs that we merely affirm, faith is holding to Christ even in the midst of extreme hardship, actually rejoicing in the pain, knowing that it leads to greater faith. Faith directs our motives. Faith leads to action. Faith gives victory.

As we learn and grow and support one another in this covenant study on faith in action, we anticipate opening new avenues in our Christian pilgrimage. Using this living document that helped early Christians support one another as the church spread into foreign territory, we will be wrangling with the problems of our own age. If James is right, our godly action will lead us to deeper faith.

So often we view the Christian life in James as only a set of instructions. We think his faith in action has too many oughts and musts. But those criticisms miss the unique spirit of James who, above all else, says "faith without works is dead." Let us put our faith in action, be "hearers and doers of the word," thus, enlivening our faith and glorifying God.

David S. Young

Recommended Resources

Barclay, William. *The Letters of James and Peter* (Daily Study Bible Series). Westminster Press, 1976.

Provides a comprehensive and easy-to-understand commentary on the Letter of James.

Davids, Peter H. *James* (New International Bible Commentary). Hendrickson Publishers, 1989.

Insightful, verse-by-verse commentary on the themes and basic message of James, which shows how early church believers used and applied the word of Jesus to their daily lives.

Tamez, Elsa. *The Scandalous Message of James: Faith Without Works Is Dead*. Crossroads.

Challenges readers not to "spiritualize" James's message, but to take seriously the tension between faith and works, wealth and poverty.

1

To Have Faith Is To Live It
James 1–5

The often overlooked Book of James is a rich letter of instruction for daily Christian living that calls us to put faith into practice.

Personal Preparation

1. Find a quiet place for meditation and read the book of James. Immediately write down your first impressions; then list any topics that challenge you. Make this the beginning of a journal that you will keep throughout the ten-week study.
2. Recall times when you felt you really lived out your faith. What made these times feel so right? Did you make any sacrifices?
3. What personal goals do you have for this ten-week study? Write these in your journal so that you can refer back to them periodically.
4. Think about the people in your covenant group and pray for each one by name.

Understanding

"To have faith is to live it." Few would disagree with this summary statement of the Letter of James. Faith, to be faith, must be put into action! But living out faith is easier said than done. How do we keep on living a Christian life when discouragement and personal trials all but ruin our faith? How do we refrain from speaking harmful words when we're more interested in adding fuel to the fire? Where do we find the genuine motivation to do a good deed when the opportunity arises? These are the questions we as Christians struggle with daily, and they are the questions that believers in James's time wrestled with, too. The Letter of James helped them, and it helps us to know how to put faith into action even in difficult times.

For James, the call of the Christian gospel is to live our faith, showing it in our actions, our motives, and our attitudes. At first, the Letter of James may seem like a collection of do's and don'ts: *do* love your neighbor, overcome temptation, be doers of the word, tell the truth, but *don't* show favoritism, don't gossip, don't conform to the world, don't be angry. In fact, Martin Luther suggested in the sixteenth century that the Letter of James should never have been included in the Bible. He called James an "epistle of straw" because it has very little theological content (*The Interpreter's Bible,* Vol. 12). But it is a rich letter of instruction for daily Christian living. It calls us to put faith into practice. While such an emphasis could degenerate into a treatise on being saved by good works, James pushes us to explore the faith and motives behind our actions. Such deep probing can be a needed corrective to a self-congratulatory attitude. James helps us to integrate faith and life. For James, to have faith is to live it!

When in seminary, my wife Joan and I had to search for a church home. God led us to a small inner-city church on the west side of Chicago, the First Church of the Brethren. We were struck immediately by the authentic faith of the people in this interracial congregation. People of diverse backgrounds and social status worked together. A day care center, mother's sewing club, youth club, and work in the nearby Bethany Hospital were all a part of the routine weekly activities. The depth of their spirituality was evident as worshipers concluded services on Sunday by asking for God's guidance in living out their faith.

When the fires of protest lit up the skies of Chicago following the slaying of Martin Luther King, Jr., active faith sustained our congregation. The period of racial tension existed just prior to Palm Sunday when the church was preparing for its semi-annual love feast that included feetwashing, an agape meal, and communion. With the National Guard patrolling the streets, we entered the church, conscious of the threat of danger. And as I knelt to wash the feet of a person of another race, I had to review the prejudice in my own heart. Washing feet, serving and being served, took on new relevance. As we took the bread and cup, our congregation was united in a faith that was real.

Practical and Active Love

When our outward actions match our inner commitment, we know an authenticity in ourselves. There is a dynamic interplay within us as faith motivates action and action leads to deeper faith. Faith, according to James, is actually made perfect through action. Ideas such as faith, patience, understanding, perseverance, and forgiveness become real. Moreover, James says, our actions show that the Spirit is alive within our hearts.

Christians who believe faith must be put into practice find a great deal of support in James. Also within the pages of James many Christians find practical teachings on peace, anointing the sick, truthfulness, the simple life, and giving a cup of cold water. The book contains as many as sixty instructions on practical Christian living. It is more than a list of oughts; it is a book of guidance on how life is lived under the design of God. James is a book of practical faith and active love.

As James directs us to put faith into action, he also challenges us to look at our motives for doing the word. Why do we do what we do? For James, undesirable results, such as prejudice toward the poor, arise out of evil motives, and bad motives lead to disorder. For instance, fierce desire causes greed and jealousy and leads to selfishness. For James, purifying our inward attitudes is the only way to produce good. Motives that come from faith produce peace and prayer and the fullness of life.

Our motives are often mixed, of course. Despite our wish to do good, we often do not do it. Paul said, "I do not do the good I want" (Rom. 7:19). James helps us see the effect of this inner confusion on outer results. We cannot live faithfully, he says, and spark the spirit of goodwill and peace when our lives are so full of tension. But James believes we can overcome the division in us. Mother Teresa is an example of a person in our day whose inner peace has led to action that affects the whole world. Whether the arena is personal or global, clear motives lead to right actions.

The fact that the Letter of James means as much to us as it did to early Christians, even though their lives were quite different from ours, testifies to its grasp of the truth. When James picked up his pen in the first century, the church was a small minority group that was just beginning to spread beyond the eastern Mediterranean into Greek culture. This group was quickly losing contact with the church centered in Jerusalem and with other Christians. As aliens and strangers in new territory, Christians faced many conflicts and hardships. They needed clear guidance on how to live out their faith in tough times.

James speaks the language of his culture, using examples from common life that would mean something to his readers. And though it is different in focus, the Letter of James teaches many of the same lessons found in the Gospel of Matthew, particularly in the Sermon on the Mount. Both tell Christians how to live practically. Both counsel the Christian to conform to an ideal greater than the law and to do more than the law requires. Both offer blessings to those who do God's will. Both contain the great commandment. Both are written for the Jewish-Christian community. That James may have been a brother to Jesus, as some scholars suggest, might explain some of the similarities in the teachings of James and Jesus.

The Joy of Living Our Lives

In the first lines of his letter, James asks the faithful who face impossible odds to endure their trials and "consider it nothing but joy" (1:2). He can ask them to make personal sacrifices because he, himself, is "a servant of God and of the Lord Jesus Christ." As a servant, he obeys the Master and serves the will of God. James promises that the test of their faith will increase their endurance, which, in turn, will make them complete and mature; and whole and perfect faith will bring them joy.

If our actions are rooted in a faith commitment, they will bring us joy, even when hardship is involved. Rather than nagging us into actions that we will do only grudgingly, leading to burnout, James empowers us to be servants who know the reason for our suffering and the source of our joy. Nurturing our faith in Christ helps us to clarify our motives and employ right actions. In the 1930s, German theologian Dietrich Bonhoeffer wrote a book called *The Cost of Discipleship*. It talks about the sacrifices that discipleship requires and the joy it gives. At the very least, discipleship entails a change of heart and faithful action. Bonhoeffer's name for faith without action is "cheap grace."

Later Bonhoeffer joined the resistance movement to the Nazis and was imprisoned by the Gestapo. A British officer who was in prison with Bonhoeffer said of him, "Bonhoeffer . . . was all humility and sweetness; he always seemed to me to diffuse an atmosphere of happiness, of joy in every smallest event in life, and of deep gratitude for the mere fact that he was alive. . . . He was one of the very few men that I have ever met to whom God was real and close" (*Letters and Papers from Prison*). Having refused emigration and safety, Bonhoeffer paid the ultimate price for his discipleship. He was executed in 1945 at Buchenwald.

Martin Luther was right. James does not dwell on theological explanations. He moves on to play out theology in the practical world. For James, "doing" the gospel completes faith. Without action, faith is not whole, theology is not finished. In James, as in the Sermon on the Mount, it is not enough to do what the law requires. It is not enough to defend ourselves, seek justice, or take an oath. Our faith enables us to go a step beyond the law to love our enemies, to be nonresistant, and to be honest without the insurance of an oath. Overall, it is not enough to merely believe the gospel; we must go a step further and fulfill the gospel, acting it out.

For Christians who migrated far from other Christians in the early years of the church, James's letter was a code to unify them. Without communication linking them together, Christians and their far-flung communities might have evaporated from world history. The church today is so large it does not fear losing touch with other Christians or fading away, but we still read James. We still need the instruction for daily life, and now, perhaps more than ever, Christians of the world need a word to unify us.

Discussion and Action

1. Share your first impressions upon reading the Letter of James. What challenging topics did people make note of?
2. Reflect on this statement, made by Ron Arnett, about James's view of faith: "To have faith is to do, to have faith is to act. To have faith is to follow the life of Jesus and to do one's best to model such a life. To have faith is to live it."

3. Name times when mixed motives have kept you from acting. Have there been times when finding a clear focus has helped you move into action.

4. Recall your personal goals for this study. Encourage one another to share these goals. Talk about how you will help each other meet your goals.

5. Think of how you will live out your faith, putting it into concrete action in the coming three months. How can your covenant group help you in this commitment?

6. Discuss the phrase "Walk and talk in the manner of love, for God is love." What could this mean for you personally? How will your covenant group walk and talk in this way?

7. Close by singing a hymn, perhaps "Spirit of the Living God," or by reading a poem that speaks to you about faith; then pray sentence prayers asking for God's leading.

2

Testing Produces Joy
James 1:2-18

James considers suffering a joy because suffering brings maturity, and in maturity we can know God deeply, a true joy.

Personal Preparation

1. In a quiet meditation time, visualize some of the hardships in your own life. Think about the word *trials*. What feelings does it bring to mind? Record memories, thoughts, and feelings in your journal.
2. Recall what helped you most during times of trials and hardship. Did the disciplines of faith have any role? Did any of the trials turn out to be blessings?
3. Read today's text and look for themes that suggest the author's perspective on facing hardship.
4. What images or feelings do these words hold for you: *joy, trials, faith, steadfastness, full, perfect, complete, lacking in nothing, crown of life*? What symbol would you choose for each word?

Understanding

Maturing in Faith Through Hardship

I work on a daily basis in the spiritual care of the terminally ill. Over and over I see the shock and anger that surface when patients learn that their lives are out of their control. Many of them ask, "Why has this illness happened to me?" Feeling a tremendous sense of loss, they come face-to-face with the meaning of life. But as I work with patients and their families, I am continually aware that faith can provide the resource people need as they face death or loss. Eventually they see that a defeatist attitude or cynicism magnifies the problem. But in faith a person can develop patience and acceptance and channel their frustration in a creative, productive way.

James feels that faith strengthens us for trials and trials help us mature in faith. Verses three and four read, "the testing of your faith produces steadfastness. And let steadfastness have its full effect, that you may be perfect and complete, lacking in nothing" (RSV). Steadfastness in this case means endurance. But endurance is not merely passive submission to pain or hardship. The person who faces calamity and realizes that one cannot change a fate such as terminal illness must actively make the choice to deepen one's faith. Growth by trial involves discipline, choices, and action.

Steadfastness under stress helps one maintain a direction toward perfection. To be perfect, according to James, does not mean a person is faultless; rather, it means a person is mature, whole, or focused. Even in the midst of crisis, people of faith have endurance to withstand pain and remain strong and whole.

Receiving the Crown of Life

James concludes this section with a beatitude: "Blessed is the man who endures trial, for when he has stood the test he will receive the crown of life which God has promised to those who love him" (1:12 RSV). When people hold on to faith during trials, they are blessed with greater sensitivity to the struggles and hardships of others. True beauty stands out to them. Important things become clear. There is a sense of victory. Some may find that they are really beginning to live.

Then James addresses the troubling question, Does God send trials to increase faith and therefore joy? Seldom do we put the words *testing* and *joy* together. Trials are something we wish to avoid. Trials signify hardship, anxiety, and pain. Feeling that we might not be in control of a situation, we become fearful and angry. How can joy be associated with such a time of testing? For James, the spirit with which we approach hardship, not the hardship itself, is what makes the difference and leads to growth in our faith. God doesn't send the curves in life; God extends a crown to those who endure the trials.

Holding to Faith in Times of Hardship

I minister to people facing extreme hardship, but even when I talk to people who have more normal lives, I see that they too have faced trauma and have chosen between cynicism and joy in response. Any one of us can become totally defeated and cynical, or we can decide to live life constructively. Many people have shared frankly with me about their trials. One person said, "Without being accused of being a fanatic, faith in God has carried me through." Another threw in this gem. "I try to look for the good in others; that is a mirror of one's own self-esteem." What a perspective! What a joy!

When James says, "Count it all joy, my brethren, when you meet various trials," he is talking about the joy produced by a faith deepened by trial. James is addressing Christians who were a minority in most places and faced persecution and torment. They also, of course, encountered the normal difficulties of life, trials that came unexpectedly. The turns and disappointments of life just happen. There is little we can do to avoid them. But for Christians, facing our stresses properly can lead to growth.

For James, the spirit with which one faces hardship makes the difference. It is not so much that suffering produces joy; rather faith produces joy that endures even suffering. The solution to handling difficulties is to face the trials of life creatively with the joyous spirit of servanthood to Christ. The perspective of faith keeps us buoyed up for every hardship that comes.

Faith as Trust in Jesus

While we vacationed in the Rocky mountains, our family was thrilled and captivated by the tundra region. Winds as high as 170 miles an hour drive off the snow at the highest elevations. In the summer, this bleak environment turns into a lovely meadow that belies a struggle for life. Even the plants have a strategy to exist in these harsh conditions. Nestled behind rocks, plants form a cushion, shielding one another. The rock breaks the wind and keeps the leaves from blowing off, protecting the vital branches. Sheltered behind granite, flowers blossom in touches of yellow, pink and orange.

In adversity, the church also grows. The individuals cling together, cushioning each other behind the rock of Jesus. When I think of Jesus' concern for us, I think of the hymn "Rock of Ages, cleft for me. Let me hide myself in Thee." We cannot escape trial but we can come to God for strength in troubled times.

When faith is weak and self-confidence is high, we are tempted to place our trust in less reliable, less durable things such as money, power, and people. Faith is knowing that God will carry us through life even when obedience to God is costly. Rather than try to avoid trials, which would be impossible, James advises readers to approach trials with an attitude of trust.

Having dealt with trials, James closes this section with thanksgiving for the blessings of life and praise for a steadfast God. He says, "Every good endowment and every perfect gift is from above, coming down from the Father of lights with whom there is no variation or shadow due to change" (1:17 RSV). Even through hardship, God's abiding light remains. God cannot be blamed. God does not lead us to temptation. God is simply there for us when something happens. We sing, "Great is thy faithfulness, there is no shadow of turning in thee." God's back is never turned on us. Does testing produce joy? Certainly not always. Testing causes dropouts, creates cynics, and makes people victims of the status quo. But faith produces joy; and trials, if we let them, increase our faith. This is the crown of God: when we are upheld, we discover the utter faithfulness of God.

Discussion and Action

1. Share some difficulty with which you have been struggling. What themes of today's session might help you see this hardship in a new light?

2. Recognize that faith as absolute trust is difficult. Write down some of the struggles and doubts that are part of your faith journey. Share these with the group.

3. Look at Psalm 30:4-12; note especially verse 5 and 11. Share times when your weeping has been turned into joy and your "mourning into dancing."

4. What are some other scripture texts that have sustained you in times of sorrow or trial? As these are shared, note them

in your journals for use in personal meditation and prayer times.

5. Do you know an individual or family in your congregation or community who is going through a time of trial? How can your group walk with them through this time? You may want to ask one or two members of your group to give further thought to this, checking with your pastor and perhaps your deacons, and then bring a recommendation back to the group.

6. Close by affirming the faithfulness of God. Share memories of God's faithfulness in times of need. Share the blessings you feel. Sing the hymn "Great Is Thy Faithfulness," and pray together.

3

Hearers and Doers of the Word
James 1:19-27

Faith is not only believing, it is doing. But for James, doers of the word do more than pray and worship. They live an untainted life and serve others such as the orphan and the widow.

Personal Preparation

1. Remember a specific time when you tried to put your faith into action. What challenges did you face? What were the results?
2. Recall a time when you tried to do a good deed but it didn't work out. What happened? Why do we sometimes miss the mark in our good intentions?
3. Read the text in several versions, if possible. Think about the phrase "doers of the word." Does it make you think of "works righteousness," or trying to save ourselves by what we do?
4. What helps you remember, even as you are a "doer of the word," that you are saved by grace?

Understanding

"Hearers and doers of the word" has a proper ring. No one would discount the need for the connection between these two things in Christian life. Yet how many of us relate what we're doing with what we've heard in the gospel? As old as the injunction may be, being "hearers and doers of the word" continues to be a fresh challenge.

True happiness is found by putting God's word into action. Happy and blessed are those who let God's word fill their hearts and then take action. People find the good life when they respond to God's word with a Christlike life of love and compassion.

Discovering the Joy of Compassion

I rediscovered the compassion and joy of doing God's word on a trip to deliver twenty Jersey heifers to Guatemala. The project began as a living memorial to a beloved person in our community who had been very involved in a 4-H club. A local family decided to honor his memory by giving a cow to a hungry community overseas through Heifer Project International. Ultimately, Heifer Project challenged our church and me specifically, saying, "How about coordinating an entire shipment of Jerseys to Guatemala?" I knew little about cows, only that each had a head and tail, gave "nature's most complete meal," and would lie down as a sign of rain.

It took a tremendous effort to put faith into action. The project involved making presentations to churches, enlisting support, collecting funds, purchasing the cows, having them inoculated, dedicating them, and finally taking them to Central America in the shell of an old propeller airplane.

The joy of doing the word came first hand when I delivered some of these animals to the remote village of San Lucas Toliman on Lake Atitlan in Guatemala. Villagers had been trained by Heifer Project to grow knee-high pasture in preparation for their new livestock. I watched the eyes of mothers as they saw the first cows come off the truck, and the priest's message was unforgettable when he gathered the villagers for worship that evening. He made the stark comparison of earthly kings, who misused people, subjecting them to hard labor, and Jesus, the new King, who has compassion, saving and serving the needy. The heifers, he said, were the work of those who followed the new King, Jesus.

Hearers of the Word

All communication begins with listening. Relationships are formed by listening. Business contracts are formed by listening. Speech and education involve listening. You might think James is giving a modern course on communication when he says, "Let everyone be quick to listen" (1:19). But the book of James speaks of listening as more than simply receiving information. James describes a life that hears and internalizes the word of God. In our urban, mobile, often frantic society, the gospel calls us to listen for the voice of God and then be doers of God's word.

The Christian life involves careful listening for God's call. The contemplative life is a way of life that listens intently for the voice of God. Evelyn Underhill, a contemplative who talks about a life permeated by God, says that when we are attentive to God's reality, we become a channel for God's work here on earth. The prayers of the contemplative do not just speak our word to God; the contemplative actively listens with sensitivity to God's word. The spiritual life means both listening to God and responding to God's word.

According to James, listening also helps us deal with emotions such as anger (1:19-21). As we become more aware of God's presence and better able to understand what strong emotions mean, we are more able to use our emotional energy creatively and faithfully. As "hearers of the word," we can redirect our anger and hatred to compassion and action for God.

Doers of the Word

If we listen deeply, actions will follow, says James.

> *For if any are hearers of the word and not doers, they are like those who look at themselves in a mirror; for they look at themselves and, on going away, immediately forget what they were like. But those who look into the perfect law, the law of liberty, and persevere, being not hearers who forget but doers who act—they will be blessed in their doing. (1:23-25)*

Mirrors were crude metal in James's time and gave people only a rough idea of their looks. For James, not much is gained if our response lasts only as long as a glance in a mirror.

The problem is that few of us believe we are guilty of this shallow faith. We think we are good Christians because we practice our religion, praying and worshiping and dutifully carrying out the rituals of Christian life. But James warns us that this is not enough: "If any think they are religious, and do not bridle their tongues but deceive their hearts, their religion is worthless" (1:26). If in our religion we profess and espouse our belief but do not listen and act, our faith is weak. Action for James does not mean that we should merely pray and worship. God requires this action: "to care for orphans and widows in their distress, and to keep oneself unstained by the world" (1:27). The simple kind of compassion James demands includes lifting up the needs of the widows and orphans, those with a natural stigma or those who feel all alone.

We can be challenged in our own lives to model faith in action. For instance, Kent Leininger is a church volunteer who went to Haiti to put his faith to work serving the people. In late September 1991 he found himself in the middle of the coup d'etat in Haiti. In a report to the church in the United States, he wrote:

> *The military continues to repress anyone suspected of supporting Aristide. Arrests without warrant, beatings, torture, and killings are becoming more and more common as the military and Tonton Macoutes become bolder. . . . In many cases, when the military learns someone they are looking for is in hiding, they will beat the rest of the family including children and grandparents to try to find his or her whereabouts. There are reports of parents being forced to beat their own children, as well as women and children being raped by the military.*

Kent had to decide whether he should leave the country for his own safety or stay to do his work. It did not take long for him to decide to stand with the Haitians, building up the faith community there. Kurt is a hearer and a doer.

Our actions may be more ordinary, but they are just as important. We may stock a food pantry for the hungry, write to a prisoner, provide shelter for refugees, or visit someone who is lonely. In any job, a Christian can demonstrate faith through simple helpfulness and a positive attitude. Even when there is tension in family life, a Christian can act to reconcile differences rather than aggravate them.

Children can be hearers and doers of the word also. Many schools are training very young children to constructively handle simple disputes on the playground, providing them with experience that will equip them to handle greater conflicts as they grow up.

Students take turns being "conflict managers," roaming the playground or looking after the classroom, making themselves available to help other students sort out their conflicts. "Managers" get parties in the dispute to agree to ground rules that include telling the truth, respecting the adversary, and being willing to work things out. Where the program is used, children prefer mediation to a trip to the principal's office! All of these daily expressions of compassion are important acts for God.

When James gave counsel to the rapidly spreading early church, he challenged them to be doers. Doers demonstrate their faith and get results. They not only pray "Thy kingdom come, thy will be done," but also they see themselves helping to make the kingdom a reality. The Christian does not grow weary by doing.

The Happy Life

Blessing comes to those who are "not hearers who forget but doers who act" (1:25). For James, happiness is found in living one's faith. An old adage says there are three cures for the blues: do something for somebody else; do something for somebody else; do something for somebody else. The gospel message provides the clearest antidote for feelings of uselessness and emptiness—faith in action.

For James, there is a freedom in hearing and doing. At the conclusion of the Sermon on the Mount, Jesus talks of the same freedom. He describes the wise man as one who builds his house on the rock and the foolish man as one who builds on the sand. The difference is that the wise man is the one who hears the words of Jesus and does them. In his obedience he is free from the threat of destruction.

The call to be doers of the word is God's invitation and challenge to us. To some, doing is a duty; to James, doing is as automatic as breathing. Listening to God's call leads one to act. And true happiness is found by putting God's word into action. The freedom to do is true joy!

Discussion and Action

1. Share times when you tried to put your faith into action. When did you have "good results"? When did things not work out as you intended?

2. Discuss this question: Since we are saved through God's grace and not through our own works, why then do we "do good works"? Because it is a law? To escape punishment?

To follow Jesus' example and teaching? Out of gratitude for what God has given? Other reasons?

3. Invite to this session someone who works with a service project or who actively lives out his or her faith. After listening and talking with this person, discuss what you have learned?

4. Explore some of the current needs around you that are unmet or ignored. Can your group work together to respond to any of these?

5. Think about something you can do each day this week that reflects your faith. Write these in your journal. Share these commitments with each other, if possible. You may want to decide on some follow-up accountability (e.g., phoning to see how commitments are being kept; sharing about this next week).

6. Share the joys you feel when you put your faith into action. Sing the hymn "They'll Know We Are Christians by Our Love," and pray sentence prayers asking God's help in living out faith.

4

No Partiality!

James 2:1-13

Since God provides abundantly for every need, we are all rich. James warns Christians about showing favor to those who have mere riches of the world.

Personal Preparation

1. Imagine the President or Prime Minister and a beggar entering your church on Sunday morning. Where would you seat them? Would you invite them to dinner? Where would you like them to eat? Then read James 2:1-13, and reflect upon your answers to the above questions.

2. Look up the commandment of love, found in Leviticus 19:18, Matthew 22:39, and Romans 13:10. How well do you think this "royal law" was followed by those who heard and later read these words?

3. Recall experiences when fair and equal treatment of others has affected your life personally. Write in your journal three practical applications of the commandment of love. Also look for instances in news reports of discrimination against the poor.

4. Remember your commitment to do something each day that reflects your faith. Keep journal notes of your actions and feelings about this project.

Understanding

A man was dressed in ill-fitting, dirty clothes and obviously had not bathed for some time. He slipped quietly into a pew just before the special advent program began that Sunday evening. Those sitting nearby looked at him disapprovingly, wrinkled their noses, and scooted farther away.

The ushers recognized the unwelcome guest. At one time he had taught in the local university. Now he lived on the streets. They walked over to him and quietly asked him to leave. He shook his head, indicating his intention to stay. The ushers withdrew to the back of the sanctuary to discuss what to do next.

The service began with music and narration. People settled back to listen with only an occasional eye turned toward the visitor sitting alone in his pew. After about ten minutes two uniformed policemen came down the aisle to where he sat. He looked up, knew why they were there, and went with them from the church. The program continued without interruption.

It is amazing how we write our own epistle by our actions. The way we treat others shows the very gospel by which we live our lives. Does our gospel shut people out of the fellowship of Christ because they do not conform to our standards? Aiming to be Christlike, we must not show partiality. We must value others equally, love our neighbor as ourselves, and uphold a compassionate view toward all people.

Clara Hale's care for drug-addicted babies in New York City exemplifies this attitude toward others that is anchored in Christ. At Hale House, Clara has taken in hundreds of infants who are born to drug addicts and who inherit their mother's habit. They are children with major health problems who face lifelong disadvantages. But Hale treats them as she would any child; she loves them.

Like Clara Hale, we want to reflect the presence of God in our lives. For James believes God's presence is nowhere more evident than in our treatment of the rich and the poor. "Show no partiality," James states. Today's English Version reads, "You must never treat people in different ways, according to their outward appearance" (2:9). Much like the opening story in this lesson, James pictures two men entering a place of worship. One man has all the trappings of wealth while the other appears in shabby clothing. The rich man has social status and is shown special distinction with a prized seat. On the other hand, the poor man is told to either stand or to sit at another's feet, that is, as a slave. Such distinctions bother James deeply because he feels discrimination arises from evil thoughts. Such attitudes lead to oppression and mistreatment and indicate that God is not present. Showing preference to the rich violates the very will of the God we are called to serve.

Clearly, James challenges us to examine what we cherish, to be more aware of our priorities and loyalties. As we go about our Christian life, we are sometimes tempted to live by the values of our culture rather than by God's values. In our consumer culture, we are easily caught up in focusing on things: clothes, cars, houses, computers, and video cassette recorders. We very subtly begin to lose our concern for those who do not have enough or those who are lonely or hard to love. We forget that they are our brothers and sisters with equal value in the sight of God. As James notes, it is they who are blessed with a deep abiding faith.

In my hospice work, I spent a great deal of time with a poor family who lived in a housing project. They encountered illegal drug activity on a daily basis in the hallways of their building. They endured sub-standard living conditions with little or no hope for escape. This family not only had to confront the realities of living but they also had to face the reality of losing their college-bound daughter who became very ill.

Having trusted in God merely to survive, they now had to trust God in order to deal with losing their daughter. Through the many hours of sharing and praying with this family, the young woman provided hope for all of us as she smiled radiantly and sang hymns. These people were truly rich in courage, love, and abiding faith.

Does the gospel put too much value on poverty? Should we all wish we were poor so we would be more virtuous? After all, Jesus condemns the rich for their sins, but in the Beatitudes, he blesses the poor who know their need for God. They are the ones, he says who will inherit the kingdom.

No, God does not love the poor any more than God loves anyone else. In this passage Jesus is trying to convince the rich that God provides abundantly for everyone. Later, in the Sermon on the Mount, Jesus offsets our anxiety over material things and our desire to control life by demonstrating that God has already provided everything we need. James suggests that the poor, who have nothing between themselves and God, naturally rely on God. The poor often learn to depend on God for true riches and this is reflected in their attitudes and priorities. As the hymn writer put it, "The riches of God are eternal."

Living the Royal Law

"You shall love your neighbor as yourself" (2:8). James calls us to love others with as much zeal as we love ourselves. The writer of Leviticus earlier lifted up this law in the Holiness Code of the Hebrew people. Faith in God is demonstrated in one's treatment not only of other Hebrews but of strangers as well. The writer points out that, after all, the Hebrews were once strangers in Egypt (Lev. 19:34); therefore, under the supremacy of God, they were to treat the stranger as a native.

Likewise, James says we must look to faith as a guide for the way we treat others. In the home, the school, the office, or factory, we face difficult situations with others. Loving others as ourselves calls us to love even in the most trying times. American theologian Reinhold Niebuhr called this way of life the "impossible possibility." He meant that while Jesus' way is difficult and sometimes impossible to implement, we should still strive for it. Flowing out of our sense of God's love for us, we can respond to others with kindness, caring, and understanding.

A young doctor in the church shared a story about how he applied this love in his work. On one occasion a family in his care became very angry with him, but he refused to respond to them in the same manner. Again and again they taunted him. Over and over, he returned love. Finding that they were unable to rile him, they remarked that they didn't know his secret. How did he stay calm? By continually using the ethic of love, the doctor witnessed to his faith and provided strength and focus in a difficult situation.

James calls this love the royal law, because it requires being kingly in manner. Kings according to their call were to be compassionate, to care for others, especially the weak, the widow, and the poor. We have a hard time thinking of ourselves as royalty. In fact, we are more comfortable thinking of ourselves as humble people. Today many people do not love themselves enough. But James says the issue is not how humble we are or how little we care for ourselves, it is *how much* we love ourselves and, therefore, how much we love our neighbor. Faith frees us from anxiety and allows us to be compassionate.

Upholding a Compassionate View

After appealing to his readers to show no partiality, James calls on them to do an even greater act: be merciful, for "mercy triumphs over judgment" (2:13). Mercy keeps us from turning the instructions in the book of James into self-righteous laws.

Almost every church has given money to a poor person who turns around and spends it on non-essentials such as liquor and tobacco. The next time someone asks for help we are then less inclined to help. How quickly we run out of mercy and become judges! Just as God has mercy over and over for our shortcomings, so should we give freely without high expectations. Jesus says that mercy extended to others is like the forgiveness we receive ourselves (Matt. 18:23-35). And the Beatitude states, "Blessed are the merciful, for they will receive mercy" (Matt. 5:7).

Certainly mercy has many meanings. Besides meaning forgiveness, the Greek word implies that the forgiving spirit moves us to compassion and doing good. Seeing the crowds in a state of helplessness, Jesus was deeply moved; he healed the sick, gave sight to the blind, and fed the hungry. *The Interpreter's Dictionary of the Bible* notes that having mercy means having the desire to help others to become whole. Faith and God's love for us create the desire within us to love God, love ourselves, and love others. Therein we are blessed!

Discussion and Action

1. Share your reflections about seating the President or Prime Minister and the beggar at your worship service and inviting them for dinner afterwards. Then write in several phrases what you think James would have written about this situation.
2. Talk about how well your congregation responds to people from different nations, cultures, races. Do you welcome, exclude, or ignore them, smile politely at them, or feel embarrassed? How can you learn to share God's love impartially, in word and deed, with all who come to church?
3. How can we learn and grow as individuals and as a congregation, by worshiping, working, and playing with people who are different from ourselves in some way?

4. What did you hear or read in news reports this week that contributes to discrimination of the poor? Share these with the group. How do such attitudes or actions deny the kind of faith James calls for?

5. Share times when fair or equal treatment of others has affected you directly (perhaps an issue related to housing, schooling, a job). Realize that the effect can be either negative or positive.

6. Share times when the presence of God has broken into your life in a special way. Thank God for such times. Then close by singing the doxology.

5

The Kind of Faith that Counts
James 2:14-26

Faith is not just a matter of accepting God's grace; true faith is a response to God's grace that includes both acceptance and action.

Personal Preparation

1. Recall a time when you saw a human need and ignored it or passed on by. Why were you reluctant to get involved?
2. Read the James text several times. Then in a time of quiet meditation, visualize your own faith; see it as being dead and you burying it. Then ask: What is needed for my faith to be fully alive again?
3. Write in your journal your feelings about a "dead faith," about your own vision of "dead faith." Write down how you will keep your own faith truly alive.
4. Read and reflect during the week on the words of the hymn "Brothers and Sisters of Mine."

Understanding

Driven by so many outside pressures and unclear motives, our actions often are not based on our faith. Our good intentions become diluted in the currents of daily life. But in James, faith and works are bonded in a unity. They cannot be separated.

As we respond to human need, live self-sacrificially, and extend hospitality, we demonstrate that our faith is alive. Like a symphony that returns over and over to a central theme, James returns to his focus on practical religion. Faith by design is practical. It is unthinkable to have faith and not live it. And doing faith involves feeding the hungry, clothing the naked, obeying God's will, and extending hospitality to others. This is the kind of faith that counts.

From Well-Wishing to Well-Doing

Encountering human need face-to-face can be an uncomfortable experience. How does one respond to the sights, sounds, and smells of hunger? I remember when I went to Guatemala City and ate at a fast-food restaurant. Children stood outside and banged on the windows. When I asked what they were doing there, someone told me they wanted my food. I could hardly finish my meal.

James approves of kind wishes for the unfortunate, but he also confronts us with the meagerness of that response. Human need is all around us. It calls for action, not just pity. Even if there are no street people living in our immediate neighborhoods, we don't have to go far to find poverty. Opportunities to put faith into action are probably right next door.

James chides us for our sanctimonious response to the needy. For example, someone sees a brother or sister in need, perhaps even someone in the church community. Unlike the religious officials in Jesus' parable of the Good Samaritan, this person does not walk by on the other side of the road. This person is sympathetic and wishes the impoverished one well. Assuming that God will take care of the down-and-out, the passerby gives a blessing. "Go in peace," he says, confident that he has done his duty. Though it may have felt good to have acknowledged the need, James says that little is gained when real action is not taken.

Our faith calls us to respond to human need, to be sensitive to others. When we are in tune with our faith, we feel uncomfortable just being well-wishers, patting people on the head as though identifying need is enough. To illustrate the type of response we can give, James provides examples of people in our midst who have immediate needs. We can help people who have physical needs (for food, clothing, shelter) or people who have emotional or spiritual needs. What about the family with alcohol and drug problems or the child who carries secrets about abuse or the woman who can't get a job because of the color of her skin? The quality of our response to such need is like a blood pressure reading on our faith.

"So it is with faith: if it is alone and includes no action, then it is dead" (2:17 TEV).

A Workless Faith

According to James, faith and works are so integrated that one cannot be considered without the other. To illustrate this connection, James turns to our understanding of God. "You believe," he says, "that God is one; you do well. Even the demons believe—and shudder" (2:19). If the demons are affected by God so much so that they shudder, how much more should we be affected. Faith is not merely intellectual assent. Faith calls for a response. For the demons there is horror and fear at the thought of God. For Christians, the response to God is faithful action.

For James, all of life is integrated; to separate faith from works that show faith is impossible. The combination, however, makes Christianity a very difficult proposition. So many pressures bear upon our lives. Attention to our own needs is still important, not to mention the time and resources needed for family, work, and church. If we really want to live our faith, where do we find the time and energy?

All of life becomes a way to fulfill our faith, for we cannot fulfill our obligation in one or two important actions. Faith is a vocation that goes on daily. That vocation is lived out in marriage and family life, on the job or as a volunteer, and in community life that includes neighbors and strangers. Doing is an outgrowth of our purpose.

We have many models who have made a vocation out of faith. Jane Addams, for instance, was a social worker and reformer in Chicago who gave up a privileged way of life to help the poor in in her city. She established Hull House, a place for the poor to get job training, housing, food, and help for community organizing. She won the Nobel Prize for Peace in 1931.

Dorothy Day founded the Catholic Worker House, a house in New York City for the homeless and hungry. Day not only organized the project, she lived in voluntary poverty with the guests at the house. And she did it in the 1930s, long before the current concern about the homeless. Since then, Catholic Worker Houses have been organized in many cities across the country.

Rosa Parks was a black woman in Montgomery, Alabama, in the 1950s. One day, exhausted after long hours of work, Mrs. Parks boarded a city bus, taking one of the front seats. When a white person got on and wanted her seat, Mrs. Parks refused to get up and move. By law, she was required to move to the back of the bus, giving her seat to any white person who wanted it. Mrs. Parks was arrested, but her supporters, including Dr. Martin Luther King, Jr., launched a whole movement to end race discrimination in Montgomery from that one small incident.

For James, a workless faith is impossible. "Show me your faith apart from your works, and I by my works will show you my faith" (2:18). To split faith and action is like having a car without an engine. It really isn't an automobile. A car is not just a body or a motor or wheels. It has to be complete to be true to its definition. James uses a pun on the Greek word for "work" to emphasize the absurdity of faith without works. In Greek, useless is rendered as "workless." So faith without works is workless.

Befriending God

This is the very heart of the human dilemma. On one hand, as humans, we want to be our own person. Our society says very clearly "look out for number one." Our government protects each individual's rights. But, as James points out on the other hand, we know we must surrender to the will of God.

Obedient living might smack of mindless submission or impossible idealism. How can anyone make a total commitment? James points to Abraham as a person whose faith was complete, full of faith and works. "Was not our ancestor Abraham justified by works when he offered his son Isaac on the altar?" (2:21). But can we achieve what Abraham achieved? Human existence is imperfect, self-serving, and unresponsive to God's call. Thankfully, God continually provides the way to deliverance. We can only do our best; we cannot justify ourselves. God must do it.

Imagine a game of checkers. God has already made a move by offering forgiveness and love. It is now our move. We are frozen on the board by our fears of inadequacy. We are trapped by anxiety and weakness. But God promises that we will be free when we respond in faithful action. In his book *Testament of Devotion*, Thomas Kelly refers to a quote by Meister Eckhart who spoke of the plenty who will follow our Lord only halfway. "They will give up possessions, friends and honors, but it touches them too closely to disown themselves." We resist the self-sacrifice it takes to obey even when we've seen how Abraham was said to be reckoned righteous. (See

Gen. 15:6.) With God as the initiator, faith is a living and active response. Such obedience earns Abraham the title "friend of God" (Isa. 41:8).

Extending Hospitality

Another example of faith that counts is found in the story of Rahab. Her faithful action was to give hospitality to the enemy. Her people hated the Israelites, but when two Hebrew spies came to her she gave them sanctuary and helped them accomplish their mission (which was deadly for her city). Rahab could have considered herself an outsider, unfit for God's work. But she chose God and God's work. This beautiful story is highlighted by Rahab's statement of faith: "The LORD your God is indeed God in heaven above and on earth beneath" (Josh. 2:11b).

James encourages followers of Christ to give hospitality, the art of tending to the needs of others. Hospitality is a sign of faith; those who have faith have ample "room" in their lives for others.

A church woman recounts her experience on the receiving end of hospitality:

> *On a visit to the Dominican Republic, a local congregation invited our American group to dinner before joining them in an evening worship service. The community butchered a lamb and prepared a special stew for us. We knew that meat in that community was very uncommon. The sacrifice of precious food, which the host community could have used for their own survival, was a special gift. Our group of six gathered in the one-room home of the pastor. Although there wasn't food enough to share with the church people, they sat with us. And because of the impure water, young boys biked several miles to purchase bottled "soft drinks" for each of us. They could only carry a few bottles on each trip, and so the soft drinks kept arriving at various points throughout the meal. How is it that our neighbors who have the least to give are the most willing to give it all, even to their wealthy guests?*

Like a body without the soul that enlivens it, faith apart from works is dead. Belief alone will not suffice; faith must be completed by works. "A body dies when it is separated from the spirit, and in the same way faith is dead if it is separated from good deeds" (2:26 JB). But when we respond to human need, live self-sacrificially, and extend hospitality, we demonstrate that our faith is alive. This is faith that counts.

Discussion and Action

1. Share times when you ignored or passed by human need. What were your feelings about that at the time? as you recall it now?
2. Talk about situations now when you feel led to respond to a specific need. What do you think you are called to do? Could your covenant group help you, or could you all work together to respond to this need?
3. Explore your understanding of God's will for your life. What do you understand as your vocation? Are your work and your family life a part of your vocation as you understand it?
4. Talk about visualizing your own faith as a "dead faith." Share what you discovered that you need in order to have an alive faith at this time.
5. Discuss hospitality as faith in action—hospitality that invites others into your life, invites them to know Christ. Where will you be so inviting this week?
6. How can you as a covenant group help your congregation practice such "hospitality evangelism" in your congregational life? in the community near your church?
7. Sing or read the words of the hymn "Brothers and Sisters of Mine" as a confession and also as your commitment. Then share with each group member where you see a living faith in action in their lives. Close with a prayer circle, offering supportive prayers for one another.

6

The Power of Words
James 3:1-12

All parts of our lives, including the way we talk, must work together for the upbuilding of the kingdom. As mature Christians, we would no more utter destructive language than a fig tree would yield olives!

Personal Preparation

1. Recall a time when you wished you could have taken back some unkind words. What feelings did you experience? How did you deal with the situation?
2. Read the text for today. Then list in your journal ways in which you might be more careful with your words. Reflect also on how your words reflect your faith.
3. What are some of the most powerful words in the scriptures for you. Write some of these in your journal.
4. Write down instances this week where you notice the power of words, both negative and positive, in speech and in writing.

Understanding

Words have tremendous power. They build up, they threaten, they persuade, they endear, and they amuse. Words such as "We hold these truths to be self evident" and "I have a dream" are tremendously empowering. Words such as "You never will be a singer" or

"You always seem to mess up" or "You are a failure" are humiliating. We have the power to use our speech for both good and bad.

Not only do words elicit good and bad emotions in us, they affect our whole lives. For instance, if someone were to tell me over and over that I am a failure, I would not only be embarrassed, I would probably become a failure.

James compares the power of the tongue to a horse's bit. In the same way that the tongue affects the whole body, a horse's bit affects the mouth and guides the horse. Similarly, the tiny rudder of the ship steers the whole great structure with and against the wind. James returns often to these themes of wholeness and connectedness. We must be hearers and doers, we must speak and act, we must pray and work. All these point to a faith in which all things work together. Otherwise we are hypocrites.

The mature Christian, whose faith and action is one and the same, will use language for the upbuilding of the kingdom. A faithful person should no more utter destructive language than a "fig tree . . . yield olives." James is scrupulously consistent in his teaching. But even he warns that we should fear perfection because "we who teach will be judged with greater strictness" (3:1).

Handling Difficult Times

The power of words is very apparent in crisis situations. I attended an employee workshop recently on how to handle difficult and tense encounters on the job. It highlighted ways to handle situations that become explosive and counterproductive. Difficult encounters emerge from differences of opinions, personality conflicts, prejudices, and workplace politics, among other things. We learned that in these situations people are tempted to start a war of words, exchanging verbal attacks in an effort to intimidate.

Our teacher noted that people often see only two alternatives in conflict resolution—fight or flight. People choose either to slug it out verbally or to run from the problem without really solving the issues. In both cases, unresolved conflict festers. We talked about a third alternative, to "flow." This technique means that one party to the conflict takes the initiative to listen, to offer empathy, and to seek options. In our workshop, we acted out responses to conflict that used the technique of flowing. Words, of course, do not have to be destructive. If used constructively, they can be part of the solution, not ammunition.

Pro-active Speech

James shows us the power of words by holding up a vocation that requires constant use of verbal skills, teaching. Teachers not only hand down a tradition, they also set the course and spirit of life. And they do it largely with words. This responsibility is a heavy one and James is quick to admit that we all make many mistakes. James includes himself when he says, "We who teach will be judged with greater strictness" (3:1).

A parents' meeting at our local high school is an example that illustrates the difficulty of using words well. The speaker opened the gathering of some seven hundred parents with these words: "How many of you told your youth today that you are proud of them?" A mother behind me muttered very audibly that she gave her daughter a message that morning, but it certainly wasn't that she was proud! Sadly, in that auditorium, not one person raised a hand. The leader then asked the parents to consider ways that encouraging comments can build positive self-esteem, thus improving motivation and creating a positive outlook. Knowing how to be encouraging—and doing it—can make all the difference in the world.

The key for James is perfection, a theme touched on in lesson one. Perfect means mature or undivided in intent and purpose. It is to be so centered in faith that our behavior reflects it. Positive speech is one product of a heart that is united with God. And for James, a controlled tongue guides the whole person to completeness and usefulness. With faith we can be a creative, positive force.

Taming the Untamable

The force that guides can also destroy. Few would disagree with James's teachings, but putting his words into practice is another matter. How do we stop from saying harmful things? If we are angry, do we count to ten before saying something? After being hurt many times, some people become cynical and sarcastic and use language to defend themselves. How can we tame the tongue and let it, in turn, tame the body? There are support groups for those who overindulge in other areas; how about a network to overcome bad verbal habits?

James, of course, has the answer to his own question: singleness of devotion and a consistency in all things. In chapter one of the letter, James says that people with devotion to things other than faith are double-minded and restless. When people are divided between faith and practice, the tongue becomes a restless evil. A unified, mature person can tame the tongue, but a divided soul cannot.

Force for God

Our speech is important for "with it we bless the Lord and Father" (3:9a). Pointing to our choices for using the tongue, James encourages us to use the voice for good. When blessing and cursing come from the same mouth, James is pained. Use the voice for constructive purposes. Let the voice witness to our devotion and servanthood to Christ. Let the voice spread the good news. Let the voice be an encouragement to others who are developing in faith. Sadly, the church can be one of the most fertile places for destructive, divisive talk; but it can also be a place for talk that builds up individuals and the congregation.

A study of five successful Sunday schools shows that people are one of seven factors that yield growth. Their positive attitudes, including speech, attract others to the church. In one church there was a man called the "candy man," not because he gave out candy to entice the children, but because he was so encouraging that children flocked to him as they would to candy. His positive behavior was a powerful influence on children. He made them want to be positive, too.

Members of the congregation are a community of faith, offering neighborliness and encouragement. Perhaps one bad apple can spoil the barrel, but one constructive individual can be a positive force who helps the whole church find unity in faith and action. We look eagerly for someone to lead us in such a constructive way. Who will be our teachers? As our faith matures, how can each of us encourage and teach others? Small group Bible study and the support of covenant groups is one way to practice faith that unifies belief and action and builds up the community. The power of words is great. May each word be in praise of God and count for good!

Discussion and Action

1. Share examples of someone's constructive words that encouraged you. Then name ways in which you could be more supportive through your words to family members, in your community, at work.

2. Recall people who, by their attractive and inviting way of speaking, have made a difference in your life, in your church.
3. Where have you heard words used for good this week? for hurt or evil? What have been the consequences?
4. Sometimes we repeatedly hear the negative voices from our past, preventing us from being all we can be. How can the power of such voices be lessened? How can we put positive messages in their place?
5. Identify some situations where you could make a positive contribution with words. Think especially of your congregational life. How can you use words more positively about your congregational leaders? about denominational leaders and programs? about your youth?
6. Share some of the scriptures that have been powerful for you. What has been the power in these particular words?
7. Use your voice to praise God, singing some familiar hymns of praise. Close by passing the peace, offering words of peace and encouragement to each group member.

7

Friendship with God
James 3:13—4:10

The manner in which we live is a reflection of our friendship with God. The better the friendship, the better the life.

Personal Preparation

1. Think about your values. Write down some of the most important values that you hold.
2. Reflect on some of the conflicting values in your life today. Which values are pulling you in several directions?
3. Read the text carefully. What do you think is the central theme of this section?
4. Reflect on verse 8 of the text, "Draw near to God, and he will draw near to you." Spend five or ten minutes each day quietly listening for God, simply being in God's presence. During this quiet time, you may wish to read the words of hymns such as "There is a place of quiet rest, near to the heart of God . . . . "

Understanding

For every person who is searching for the good life, there are others, it seems, who think they can offer it: doctors, manufacturers, politicians, bankers. For years Americans have believed that the good life is one that indulges their personal desires. In fact, the 1980s, with its materialism, instant gratification, and fast-track careers, were dubbed the "me decade." But this kind of life leaves people empty, angry, and unhappy.

Time magazine reveals a change in the 1990s, the "we decade." People now focus more on simple pleasures, caring for neighbors, and developing their spirituality. Their values include a devotion to family, volunteerism, and community involvement. They are searching again for meaning in their lives.

In James we find that the good life comes from friendship with God and is demonstrated in peaceable living. The good life is a life of wisdom. It is not the wisdom of advertisements, fast-track values, or a secular society, but the wisdom of the gospel. For James, the good life is the result of our friendship with God in whom we place ultimate trust and who gives us peace.

Double-mindedness or Wisdom

How to attain wisdom is an endless debate. Who is wise? Often in James's society, as in ours, wisdom was gleaned from the wrong sources and resulted in the wrong kind of action. As James suggests in his opening chapter, the opposite of wisdom is not ignorance; it is doubt. Doubt, for James, is not so much a matter of intellectual questioning but, rather, mixed-up loyalty to the things of this world, which lead to action that is not always godly. The notion that we can have it both ways, that is, that we can love both God and the world, is what James calls double-mindedness.

Wisdom, on the other hand, is life lived in wholeness with God. The wise are undivided in their loyalty to God. The wise have a singular purpose. The wise rely on God's logic, which is opposite the world's logic. Lifting up meekness, James points to the wise way of humility, a way that is often ridiculed in our culture which associates humility with slavery and weakness. In a power-conscious culture such as our own, the wisdom of the world says we should protect ourselves and our own self-interests. For James, this is precisely why we experience the kind of jealousy and selfish ambition that lead to confusion and meanness. True wisdom is a gift from God and is characterized by meekness and humility. To be wise is to be continually open to the will of God.

Thos who place an abiding trust in God receive "wisdom from above [that] is first pure, then peaceable, gentle, willing to yield, full of mercy and good fruits, without a trace of partiality or hypocrisy" (3:17). Peace is not just a distant wish but is already being implemented in the life of wisdom. "And a harvest of righteousness is sown in peace for those who make peace" (3:18).

The Peaceable Life

From Church of the Brethren history comes a story of a wise farmer. This farmer was thinking of buying a certain parcel of land. He was told that the man who farmed on the neighboring land had so contested the property line that the former owner sold out. No sooner had the farmer moved in when the neighbor came to tell him that the fence had to be moved. The farmer asked, "Where should the line be?" And he then insisted that the line be set to the advantage of the neighbor so that there would be total satisfaction. The value of the little strip of land was minor compared to good relations with his neighbor. Seeing how fair the farmer was, the disgruntled neighbor said, "We'll leave that fence where it is." However, this was not to end all problems.

One day the farmer's cattle broke into the neighbor's cornfield, damaging the crop. The neighbor flew into a rage and declared he would sue the farmer. Calmly the farmer explained that this would not be necessary. He was ready to pay in full. Rather than incur court costs, he suggested they engage a third party to settle on a suitable remuneration. Seeing the peaceful nature and honesty of the farmer, the neighbor asked, "Why choose others to arbitrate? We can settle that ourselves. There are no damages. The matter is settled. I never before met a man like you. No one can quarrel with you."

From this perspective, James asks a simple question, "Those conflicts and disputes among you, where do they come from?" (4:1). Why do people kill one another on the interpersonal or international level? For James, the separation of faith and practice causes us to destroy others and ourselves. Jealousy, conflicting desires, and selfish cravings cause people to come to blows. James says even our prayers are a source of conflict when petitions are made up of selfish requests such as patriotic prayers that ask for victory for us and death to the enemy. Craving the good life, as the world sees it, creates confusion and animosity. The outer war, so to speak, is a manifestation of the inner war.

In a statement on peace with justice, the Disciples of Christ talk about God's peace and the world's peace. "There has been wide affirmation that the pursuit of peace with justice is a biblically and theologically mandated task of paramount importance for the church. When the numbers of starving people are rising, national antagonisms remain at the tinder-point, and global militarization is increasing, the temptation often is to give in to a sense of helplessness and apathy about the world, to turn inward and care only for oneself." Seeking true peace is an act of faith whose goal is reconciliation, not victory or revenge.

The life of peace originates out of a basic friendship with God that reflects God's spirit in our manner of living. The Church of the Brethren has said, "Peace is life in God's spirit, the same spirit that gave birth to creation and breathed life into the clay we are, that dwelt in Jesus whom Christians know as Savior, and that unites in holiness all who live by God's spirit" (*Peacemaking,* Annual Conference, 1991).

James asks the question plainly. Will we be friends of the world or friends with God? Our constant search for pleasure exposes our basic mistrust in the promise that true happiness comes from God. The responsibility rests with us; only we can appoint ourselves as an enemy of God. Only we can choose the wisdom of the world over God's wisdom. Faith calls for a cleansing of the heart and a mending of divisions. While in some traditions people take their confessions to a priest who goes to God on their behalf, James tells us that repentance and making amends with God is everyone's responsibility and opportunity. The wise person who wants to overcome the divisions in loyalty will choose to be a friend of God. Trusting in God to bring happiness will heal the soul of its double-mindedness.

The Exalted Life

What James says may run counter to what we feel is practical. While we are trying hard to live as God would have us, we may wonder why the crooks get all the breaks. Why is it that those who cause the most distress make the front page? There does not seem to be much glory in humility, and there is very little gratitude for sacrifice. After all, human nature doesn't naturally follow the contours of friendship with God. Why should we even try?

As a child, I would sometimes hear the expression "Great will be your reward in heaven." I often felt that such a reward seemed so far off! In a culture of instant gratification, the Christian life is an investment for the long haul. God does lift up the humble, giving them strength, grace, and a unique beauty. As Jesus said in the Beatitudes, "Blessed are the meek for they will inherit the earth"

(Matt. 5:5). Humility and surrender provide the most resources for the inner strength to face life's greatest hardships and trials. Humility makes us strong! Humility is the posture of faith, because God can draw near to us and lift us up.

The good life of faith, with all of its humility, obedience, self-sacrifice, and denial, is not a joyless, dreary life. We are not doomed to a monastic life because we have made a commitment to Christ. Humility gives us great confidence that we are God's children; obedience makes us absolutely free; self-sacrifice brings us an abundance of what we need; and rejection of the fragile promises of this world leads to joyful acceptance of God's love and grace. The good life is a great life!

Discussion and Action

1. Share how it was for you to spend quiet time each day "abiding in God." Then name times you have known God "drawing close to you."
2. Share some of the most important values you hold. Does anyone list "friendship with God" as a high value?
3. Discuss some of the conflicting values you experience in your life.
4. Consider James's unique view of conflict and war. Where do you agree or disagree with his analysis? How have you experienced conflict with friends?
5. What is your own personal call to peacemaking? What is your church's call and commitment to peacemaking?
6. Close with a time of silent, listening prayer. You may want to use the words of a prayer hymn, spoken quietly as a prayer, or sing a prayer hymn to close your prayer.

8

Rejecting God
James 4:11-17

The good life begins by renouncing our disobedience to God. James identifies four sins of disobedience: slander, profiteering, arrogance, and neglecting to do the right thing.

Personal Preparation

1. Read the text, and note the four sins of which James calls us to repent: slandering and criticizing others; over-valuing profit and possessions; boasting in arrogance; neglecting to do justice.
2. Have there been times when making money and accumulating things became too important in your life? How do you find the appropriate place for money and possessions in life?
3. Be aware of words, yours and others, that unjustly criticize or tear others down. Confess times when you have misused words.
4. Pray prayers of confession this week—confessing the four sins that mean rejection of God in our life. Also pray intercessory prayers for each member of your covenant group.

Understanding

In our modern culture with its many conflicting values, people are searching for whatever leads to happiness. In their book *Fulfilling Lives,* Douglas and Harriet Heath talk about the things that make for real happiness. They conclude that happiness comes from being more other-centered, more committed, and more self-disciplined. These values resemble James's list of virtues that make up a godly life. Yet, even when we know these virtues will produce happiness, we more often choose the wisdom of the world, rejecting God's counsel and rejecting God in the process.

We have already looked at wisdom's way, a life that is undivided by the conflicting demands of our world. Now James moves from a general call to live the good life to the practical instructions for living in partnership with God. Specifically, to live a life of faith we must repent of four sins of disobedience: slander, profiteering, arrogance, and neglect of doing right.

Slander

"Do not speak evil against one another, brothers and sisters. Whoever speaks evil against another or judges another, speaks evil against the law and judges the law; but if you judge the law, you are not a doer of the law but a judge" (4:11-12). This is James's counsel on avoiding the endless criticism of others, otherwise known as slander and detraction. Slander is a serious sin because it demeans other people and it blasphemes God. By judging others, we impersonate the one and only judge. "Who . . . are you to judge your neighbor?" (4:12).

When we talk, we easily turn to criticism of others. As harmless as private conversations seem, words can tear people apart. Endless amounts of time and energy are spent tearing down other people. And sadly, people who try to make themselves look good by making someone else look bad have little virtue on which to base their own superiority. James specifically warns against defaming others to build our own reputations. Unless our speech is constructive, little is accomplished.

In his *Introduction to the Devout Life,* St. Francis de Sales offers these words written in 1608:

*Be careful never to let an indecent word leave your lips,
for even if you do not speak with an evil intention those*

who hear it may take it in a different way. An evil word falling into a willing heart grows and spreads like a drop of oil on a piece of linen cloth.

Critics sin against others when they put people down, but they also sin against God's law. James's prohibition against slander is similar to the Levitical law of love of neighbor (Lev. 19:18); and criticism of another violates this fundamental code. God alone is the lawgiver and judge.

Profiteering

A second concern of James is profiteering. There were those in the early church who went from town to town to make money. They thought only of their own gain and didn't put anything back into the community. At their worst, we would call them flimflam operators. James criticizes them for building up caches of money. He said, "You do not even know what tomorrow will bring. What is your life? For you are a mist that appears for a little while and then vanishes" (4:14). Like those who build a reputation on the dubious base of slander, the greedy base their existence on a wobbly foundation of money.

A cartoon in the *Christian Century* magazine pictured Noah's ark with the gangplank down to receive the animals. Two by two they go into the ark. But instead of two of each animal, there were two toasters, two blenders, two fans, two mixers—all signs of an era that has focused on accumulating things rather than caring for people and the earth.

People are growing weary of the money game. The news has carried stories about people leaving lucrative jobs to spend time with their children. One person interviewed said that at the close of his life he knew he would not be saying, "I wish I had spent more time at the office." Making money has its place, but we must remember that our vocation is God working through us; it is not a way to amass a fortune.

Again, James ridicules us. The profits we revel in and depend upon are only temporary, he says. "Your riches have rotted, and your clothes are moth-eaten. Your gold and silver have rusted, and their rust will be evidence against you, and it will eat your flesh like fire" (5:2-3). The very thing we think will save us is the thing that will destroy us.

Arrogance

A third area of concern for James is arrogance. Arrogance is a self-appointed importance that makes us believe we are in control of life. In our society, control has become very important. People want assurances for their future, their property, their health, and their success. But James tells us, "As it is, you boast in your arrogance; all such boasting is evil" (4:16).

"Instead," James says, "you ought to say, 'If the Lord wishes, we will live and do this or that' " (4:15). The proper credit for control always belongs to God. When we struggle with a decision, we must ask God for guidance. After all, our decisions are for God, not for our own benefit. Clarity comes as we yield control to God in our lives. One advantage of a regular prayer life is that we can discipline ourselves to ask God to help us make decisions that God would have us make. When we are unclear about what we want in life, we should seek God's will for us.

In the closing chapter of the book *The Will of God*, Leslie Weatherhead describes how God's will is our security. God creates direction for us out of the circumstances in which we find ourselves. We are like the swallow who finds her way from Africa through storms and driving winds to the same little village church where she built her nest the year before. Rather than fretting, we gain the courage and trust to find our way, knowing that the living God will bring clarity and fulfillment.

Neglecting Justice

Finally, James condemns knowing what is right and failing to take action. For him this is as great a sin as doing the wrong action. "Anyone then, who knows the right thing to do and fails to do it commits sin" (4:17).

In his book *Everything to Gain*, former president Jimmy Carter tells how he knew what was right and did it. Just after his defeat in the presidential election and the release of American hostages in Iran, Carter returned to his hometown only to find his personal finances devastated. The world around him was crashing down and he faced a "potentially empty life." Late one night he sat upright in bed with the words "conflict resolution" in his mind. This was the beginning of what would eventually become the Carter Center for Conflict Resolution, where parties and nations are invited to work out differences peacefully. Jimmy Carter is now in great demand as a conflict mediator. Seeing the right thing and doing it helped him rebuild an otherwise defeated life.

Wisdom's way is being a hearer and doer of God's will. In doing God's will, we are to reject slander, profiteering, and arrogance, and do the right thing in order to have peace and purpose. In the end, sin is not just the result of doing the wrong thing. It is the result of failing to do the right thing. Faith without works is dead. Worse yet, faith without action is a sin.

Discussion and Action

1. Share times when you have rejected God by slandering another person, over-valuing money and profits, being arrogant, or failing to do justice. Name these confessionally and prayerfully; do not criticize or judge each other's actions.

2. Name some common ways we hear people criticizing or putting other people down. For each example, think of ways you could respond that would be helpful.

3. Discuss the importance of making money and accumulating things in your life. When do our money and possessions indicate sinfulness?

4. The writer names the human need to "be in control" as part of the sin of arrogance. Where do you find yourself wanting such control? How do you seek to turn control over to God? What does it mean when you say "the Lord willing"?

5. Record in your journal times when you have "known what is right, but failed to do it," thus sinning and rejecting God. Share these notes if you care to.

6. Close by reading together or listening as one person quietly and prayerfully reads the words of the hymn "Have Thine Own Way, Lord." Or sing the hymn as a closing prayer of commitment.

9

Doing While Waiting
James 5:1-11

What we do while we wait for the fulfillment of the kingdom is important, for the kingdom will bring with it the judgment of the just and the unjust.

Personal Preparation
1. Reflect on what you do when you have to wait. Do you bring something to the waiting time, or do you just fret?
2. Recall a time when someone was patient with you. Write a thank you note in your journal; or write a personal note to the person and send it.
3. Read the text for this session once a day; spend some time in quiet reflection following each reading.
4. Are you or another member of your covenant group facing a difficult situation? If so, bring it to God in prayers of petition or intercession this week.

Understanding
What do you do while you're waiting? Observe each of the shoppers in the check-out lane in the supermarket to see how impatient people are. No doubt, some are tempted to leave the groceries without checking out. Recall how it feels to get tied up in traffic. Some people become agitated and get out of their cars; others blow their horns. Watch hungry children as they wait for dinner and you will see all kinds of reactions. Who likes to wait?

Waiting is an important topic in the book of James. Christians of James's time believed that Jesus would return soon and that they should be prepared to usher in the kingdom in all its fullness. What do we do while we're waiting for the kingdom? Nearly 2000 years have passed and we are still waiting. How does the church remain faithful when the rewards of the kingdom are not so imminent? Should we keep trying to implement the Christian way even though we will not witness the fulfillment of the kingdom in our lifetimes? Perfection is impossible, so who would blame us if we allowed the values of our culture to influence our lives?

James urges us to be patient and to wait steadfastly as the farmer who waits on the early *and* the late rains (5:7). What we do in the meantime is important, for the coming of the kingdom will bring with it the judgment of both the unjust, who will be condemned, and the just, who will be rewarded. All will be accountable for their actions in this waiting period. A woman having her picture taken for her drivers license was objecting to having to smile for the photographer. "I won't be smiling when the trooper stops me," she said. With quick wit the photographer replied, "That's only if you were breaking the law. Otherwise you would be happy to see your friendly trooper."

Some people believe the promise of the Second Coming relieves them of having to strive for the kingdom. But according to James, it is the record of our living in these times that will determine our fate in the end. The only ones who are secure are the ones who live as if the kingdom were already here.

Living with Right Values

While waiting, we are tempted to get caught up in the secular values of our society, sometimes confusing social values with religious ones. In fact, in a materialistic culture, people often see prosperity as a sign that God favors them and is rewarding them. After all, money makes us happy and God wants us to be happy. A number of years ago at Northwestern University, researchers studied lottery winners who suddenly received great fortunes. At first winners felt that it was one of the best things that ever happened to them. However, they reported that their actual level of happiness did not increase. In fact, daily activities such as reading or eating breakfast became less pleasurable. Like an addict, it took more and more to satisfy. A psychology of affluence can leave us empty.

In the same way that a drug gives pleasure to the addict until it takes over and begins to destroy the body, our injustices eventually turn on us. James says,

Come now, you rich people, weep and wail for the miseries that are coming to you. Your riches have rotted, and your clothes are moth-eaten. Your gold and silver have rusted, and their rust will be evidence against you, and it will eat your flesh like fire. You have laid up treasure for the last days. Listen! The wages of the laborers who mowed your fields, which you kept back by fraud, cry out, and the cries of the harvesters have reached the ears of the Lord of hosts. You have lived on the earth in luxury and in pleasure; you have fattened your hearts in a day of slaughter. You have condemned and murdered the righteous one, who does not resist you. (5:1-6)

God judges the unjust with or without the Second Coming. Consider, for example, the consequences of injustice in South Africa in our own era. Violence and sorrow plague both the just and the unjust now, not only in the future.

In yet another reference to Matthew, James cautions us against banking our treasures for the future and the last days. Any attempt to stave off poverty by hoarding riches constitutes robbery from others and robbery earns us condemnation. Once again the sin finds us out eventually.

The life of waiting must be modeled after the kingdom. While we wait, we must actively focus on Jesus and our faith. Anything else is secondary. This means giving kingdom interests priority, centering our trust in God, and finding our enjoyment in a world rich with natural beauty. Also it means becoming sensitive to those who have less than we do. Several decades ago a pastor wrote a formative piece on the simple life. He asked the timely question:

How can I live in a skeptical age, immersed in luxuries and nurtured in extravagance, surrounded by hungry and homeless people all over our globe, and still be true to the Spirit of Christ? . . . Luxury invites men to comfort and pleasure. Jesus called men to live a humble, simple life.

How can we live by the simple life and avoid the values and behaviors of an affluent culture? For one, we may choose to buy a washing machine with fewer features and give the savings to a local mission for clothing. Instead of purchasing the most recent model of VCR, we can give to a project that feeds the hungry. As a family, we may decide to take a walk for exercise and visiting rather than going shopping in the mall. Most of all, the simple life requires that we focus on faith, reducing the clutter in our lives so we have more time for the kingdom. In whatever way we spend our time waiting, we should remember that waiting is not a waste of time. It is an action.

Using the imagery of agriculture, James points to the farmer who plants the crop and waits for the two major rains of the season. Patience is not just enduring but anticipating. Patience is an active trust, a confidence that God will look favorably on our work and be gracious with the harvest.

For James, the prophets model living a kingdom life while patiently waiting for fulfillment. Prophets live out their beliefs and speak their convictions regardless of the consequences. Writing about the life of Dan West who founded Heifer Project International, Glee Yoder says, "Dan was a prophet. Prophets are 'why' people, not 'how' people. Like an itinerant Johnny Appleseed, he moved about spreading the seeds of goodwill and peace." Baptized at a young age, Dan was deeply committed to Jesus Christ, not just in theory, but as one who patiently and persistently worked to fulfill his dreams. He did not merely plan for the future or hope for salvation, he "established" his heart. He went to work immediately, throwing in his lot with God and living out the kingdom in the here and now.

Expressing Mutual Support

When patience turns to impatience and people doubt that God's plan will ever be fulfilled, we give in to the "cravings that are at war within [us]" (4:1). Disillusioned about idealistic biblical promises, we resort to old ways of living. We are cruel to others. We look for someone else to blame. Stress from double-mindedness and uncertainty about our relationship to God makes us weary. James encourages us to endure longer and resist grumbling about each other.

Living Steadfastly by Faith

Living steadfastly is the challenge of faith. In whatever position we find ourselves, whatever occupation, whatever endeavor, a singular dedication to God will finally carry us through. If we live a Christ-centered life, we will have purpose in our life that is a blessing to others. Honesty, patience, and love will stand us in good stead.

As an illustration, James points to the steadfastness of Job. Job's so-called friends criticized him, assuming he was suffering because he did something to deserve it. But Job remained faithful to God through thick and thin, and in the end he was found faithful. God has compassion and mercy for those who persevere. Without ever knowing the time or the place in which the kingdom will come, we already know that God blesses us in our waiting. How much more will be the blessings in the fullness of time.

Discussion and Action

1. Share memories of people who were patient with you. Recall and share times when you have been patient in a trying situation and times when you have been impatient.
2. What does "waiting for the kingdom to come" mean to you? What do you think you are called to do during this waiting time?
3. What do you think of when you hear the word *steadfast?* Imagine *steadfast* as a color. What color would it be for you? Tell others your color choice and the reasons for your choice.
4. In what parts of your life do you think you are steadfast? In what circumstances is it hard for you to stand firm or be steadfast?
5. Discuss the report showing that happiness does not come as a result of lottery winnings. Can you name instances when affluence has not brought happiness to people?
6. What does "living the simple life" mean to you, as you live in the kingdom of God, waiting for the full kingdom to come?
7. Pray sentence prayers, asking God's guidance as you learn to wait and work; close with the Lord's Prayer. You may want to listen to a recording of this prayer or sing it together as your prayer.

10

The Healing Community
James 5:12-20

*James counsels the church to prepare for the coming of
the kingdom by living a life of truthfulness, healing,
prayer, and restoration of the lost.*

Personal Preparation

1. Read through your journal entries from this ten-week period, and reflect on what this study of James has meant for you. How well have you met the personal goals you set? Do you feel a closer kinship to biblical people and to others in your group?

2. Read James 5:12-20. Reflect on times when prayers for healing, or perhaps anointing for healing, have been part of your life.

3. Record in your journal any situations where you desire healing now.

4. Spend time in quiet meditation and prayer. Pray for healing for yourself, for others, for specific situations in the world. Pray also for openness to God and to others in your life.

Understanding

As James closes his letter to the Christians who are migrating far from Jerusalem, he gives one last piece of advice to the church. He instructs Christian communities everywhere to live in the confident hope of the coming of the Lord and to ready themselves to be the messianic kingdom in the meantime. James says the church should prepare in four ways: by living a life of truthfulness, a life of healing, a life of prayer, and a life of reclaiming the lost. As the church, we are the living expression of the power and presence of Christ at work. This is how our membership, our mission, and our calling are defined.

A Life of Truthfulness

Do not take oaths. "Say only 'Yes' when you mean yes, and 'No' when you mean no," James says (5:12 TEV). The taking of oaths was a common religious practice of the day. It was a way to insure truthfulness. However, the need for oaths indicated that straightforward promises were not trustworthy and consequences were needed to reinforce the pledge. For instance, I might swear that the gods strike me dead if my story is not true. Rather than use religion as a threat, James instructs us to let yes be yes and no be no.

Memories come back to me of the car dealer from whom I purchased my first automobile. Having looked at a Plymouth Valiant station wagon and taken a test drive, I asked for the price and he gave me a figure. When I returned the next day to purchase the car, the owner claimed that he had quoted a higher price the day before. He would swear to it on a stack of Bibles. Having come from a faith tradition that does not take oaths, I explained how I had been taught to be truthful. He paused for what seemed like the longest moment and said, "I'll sell the car at the price originally quoted." One mark of a faith community is utter truthfulness, which stands out against the prevalence of lying. There is no need for backing up the truth. Deception is characteristic of the world, but truthfulness is a hallmark of the kingdom.

A Life of Healing

James's second instruction for the messianic community is to take on a ministry of healing. This concept is central to the definition of *church*. We are the *ekklesia* or called-out-ones to bring healing and wholeness. In the midst of a broken world, James sees the mission of the church to be a healer who works under the power of Christ. In *Weavings* magazine, Avery Brooke links the martyrdom of early Christians with healing: "To early Christians the joyous abandon of Christians in the arena was directly related to healing because whether facing death with joy or receiving healing through prayer, it was Christ's power and presence that accompanied the task."

We remember these familiar words: "Are any among you sick? They should call for the elders of the church and have them pray over them, anointing them with oil in the name of the Lord" (5:14). Commending believers to confess their sins to one another in a service of anointing clears the way for physical and spiritual restoration.

Oil was widely used for medicinal purposes and also for anointing. Anointing with oil is a rich blessing noted in the 23rd Psalm and is used in the miracles of healing performed by the twelve disciples (Mark 6:13). Anointing and prayer served the sick and broken; they also benefitted the entire church, which was made whole again by the restoration of its member.

The anointing is a cherished practice in the Church of the Brethren. An individual may request anointing for physical, emotional, and relational healing. The anointing opens the way toward restoration which includes, but goes beyond, the physical.

The service usually brings deep inner peacefulness and a sense of God's presence. In his booklet *Anointing,* Dean Miller refers to the many uses of anointing in a congregation's ministry of healing and reconciliation: "Partners in a marriage are anointed as they work through the tension and anguish of a strained relationship. Someone who has lived through the painful illness and death of a spouse now looks toward anointing as a resource for the healing of heart wounds. A critically ill cancer patient, within weeks of death, is anointed primarily for the sense of feeling the reality of God's forgiveness. Another who has been abandoned in a relationship requests anointing as an aid in the healing of memories." The church has a special mission to be a healing community helping a broken world become whole in the name of Jesus. Prayers of faith and anointing for healing are an important part of this mission.

A Life of Prayer

At the heart of the messianic community is prayer. As an example, James points to Elijah, a prophet who demonstrated strength because he came to trust in "a voice of gentle stillness." He prayed on Mount Carmel that God would send a sign to show that the world was not under the dominion of fertility gods but wholly in God's hands. For James, Elijah is an ordinary person just like us. We can pray as fervently and be as faithful. God will hear our prayers and respond.

Prayer is an important act of faith for James. Prayer commits us to a mission and empowers us. My grandmother modeled that kind of prayer for me. She lived her religion so that one could see it in her face. I remember peering through the bars of the crib to see her in prayer. Once when I was older, she showed me a picture in her well-worn Bible of the prophet Elijah being fed by the ravens during the drought. How people of prayer are drawn together over the span of generations! They draw strength from one another. Prayer is at the heart of the church. Otherwise we become tired, burned out, and unfocused. Prayer gives us power!

Often people ask how to pray; at times simple prayers are best. Just a sentence declaring our trust in God can give that sense of God's presence in our lives. One of the most deeply moving prayers I have ever heard had only one word. We were at a camp for youth with physical handicaps. When time came for grace at the picnic, I thought a counselor would offer the words. But the leader called up a young handicapped boy to pray. The crowd of thirty soon became totally silent. In a moment there was that gentle stillness of Elijah and then the one word came: "Amen." God's presence was there as love, and the love of the people was real. What power!

Reclaiming the Lost

James finishes his book of practical Christianity by offering words on reclaiming the lost. Since we've seen the parallels between James's Letter and Matthew's Gospel, it is interesting to note the contrast between Matthew's ending which features the Great Commission and James's ending which calls for reclaiming the lost. Here the intent is to draw back those who have left the church community. In other words, the Christian community never stops caring for one another. The act of regaining a person has a mutual benefit since it covers the sins of the person who is reclaimed as well as the ones who do the reclaiming.

Since my ministry carries me into the wider society on a daily basis, I have come to a new understanding of restoration. People who have experienced some brokenness in the church are extremely receptive to ministry, often yearning deeply for the life of community offered by the church. However, they wait for the church to come to them. Too often the church also waits. But James essentially tells the church to go to them; no one said this is an easy job.

During an early morning walk with my wife, our conversation turned to a discussion of restoring members. "The difficulty with reclaiming the lost," she said, "is that it drives us back to our very purpose as the church." "That's what James is saying," I said. She replied, "Yes, but it is harder to reclaim the inactives because then we have to face what caused them to leave in the first place." This is the concern that James is addressing. He says that the inroads of sin drive people away from the fellowship.

While it is not easy to face old wounds, we can forgive sins and allow healing to occur. The good news is that God does not abandon us. Once our hearts are changed, God can use our inadequate gestures to bring healing for others. Let us be this healing, messianic community, demonstrating faith in action!

Discussion and Action

1. Share what this study of James has meant for you personally and for your covenant group.
2. Describe an experience when you were tempted not to tell the truth. How did you resolve the conflict? Why is truth-telling important to you now?
3. Share experiences when healing has occurred, both for yourself and for others. If people have been anointed or have participated in an anointing service, relate some of these experiences.
4. Since reclaiming a lost person is often harder than gaining a new one, discuss the possibility of forming teams to visit someone who is inactive in your congregation. Discuss how you will do this, including talking with your pastor and possibly the deacons. What follow-up might your covenant group want to do?
5. Since prayer is so much a part of James and of a covenant group, offer prayers of support for one another. Invite people to share prayer needs; then pray for each one by name, perhaps with laying on of hands.
6. An anointing service would make an appropriate closure, if someone has a particular need. (See suggestions in the Sharing and Prayer section for such a service.) The hymn "Anoint Us, Lord" could be used as part of the service or as a closing prayer for this Bible study.

Suggestions
For Sharing and Prayer

This material is designed for covenant Bible study groups who spend one hour in sharing and praying together, followed by one hour of Bible study. Some suggestions are offered here to help relate your sharing to your study of *James: Faith in Action*. Session-by-session ideas are given first, followed by general resources. Use the ones you find most helpful. Also bring your own ideas for sharing and worshiping together in your covenant group. June Adams Gibble, Elgin, Illinois, compiled this guide.

1. To Have Faith Is to Live It

□ Introduce yourself and tell others in the group about people you remember from childhood or your youth who truly "lived their faith."

□ Keep a journal to record thoughts, reflections, and feelings from your personal study and ideas gleaned from the group's time together.

□ Talk about ways your covenant group can express faith in action. James talks about faith as very concrete action; therefore, consider taking on a special project: recycling waste, collecting food and other items for food pantries, participating in soup kitchens or shelters for the homeless, working on special projects for elderly people, inviting friends or others from your community to church or to your group.

□ Consider inviting a covenant group in another church to be your "sister covenant group."

□ Discuss the possibility of establishing a "sister city" relationship between your community and a Russian city. See suggestions given in "General Sharing and Prayer Resources."

□ Plan for prayer partners (two people to share with each other about their lives, to share requests for prayer, to pray

together). Today, after prayer partners are chosen and have
talked awhile, pray together "Teach Us to Pray" (p. 73) and
then pray specifically for each other.

2. Testing Produces Joy

❑ Share some feelings from early school years that you
remember about times when you were tested by adversity or
other challenges. Were you more receptive to some testing
than to others?

❑ Name some of the people who have helped you through
times of trial, of testing in your life.

❑ Share with prayer partners any special needs for prayer at
this time; spend time praying with and for each other.

❑ Share with the total group some of the hymns that have
sustained your faith through trials and adversities; sing some
favorites.

❑ Learn the hymn "My Life Flows On" (p. 75), and use it as
your statement of faith and joy. Sing it as a group, or have
one person sing the stanzas and all join in on the refrain.

3. Hearers and Doers of the Word

❑ Invite others to share food with your group—perhaps some
children, the youth from your church, or elderly people who
are often alone. Share a light meal, sing together, and close
by singing the covenant song "Weave," if you have a copy.

❑ Make a group collage, using photos, pictures, news stories
that speak of our world's need for "doers of the word." Bring
these in from magazines, newspapers (even worship bulletin
covers). Give your finished work a title/theme ("Be ye doers
of the word" or some other text from James).

❑ Consider how our care of creation, of God's world, reflects
"doing the word." Use the video "The Earth Is the Lord's"
(order from Brethren Press, 1-800-323-8039). You may find
additional ideas in the newsletter "Between the Flood and the
Rainbow" (see "General Resources").

❑ Pray together, using the litany "Come, Holy Spirit, Renew
the Whole Creation" (p. 72). Close with the Lord's Prayer.

4. No Partiality!

❑ Recall times in your childhood when you felt that somebody was a "favorite" and you were not; share some of these memories and feelings.

❑ Bring to the group a collection of news stories and pictures that speak about or show partiality, prejudice, racism, preferences related to wealth and poverty. Make posters or a group collage. Then reflect on the message that is being spoken to you through these visuals.

❑ Look in your hymnal for songs that speak to issues of partiality, prejudice, racism. Read them or sing an appropriate one as a prayer of commitment. Or learn the hymn "Brothers and Sisters of Mine" (p. 76) and use that as your prayer.

5. The Kind of Faith That Counts

❑ Remember some times when you really wanted "to count for something" or times when you felt you "didn't count for much."

❑ Talk about the kind of faith that really "counts for something" today.

❑ Consider using a video that portrays such faith. Several sections from "Journey In Jesus' Way" would be good. This title may be ordered from Brethren Press (1-800-323-8039). Or call your denominational offices for other suggested titles.

❑ Read the words of "Brothers and Sisters of Mine" (p. 76), one stanza at a time; follow each reading by singing the words. Then pray sentence prayers asking for the kind of faith that responds with love to the needs around us.

6. The Power of Words

❑ "Sticks and stones may break my bones, but words will never hurt me." Do you remember hearing this jingle when you were a child? What was the situation? What do you think about it now?

❑ Use your time to write notes of encouragement or cards of thanks and appreciation to people.

- ❏ Name the positive gifts you see in each member of your covenant group. You may want to give a special "thank you" to each other or to your prayer partner. A People of the Covenant mug, filled with some treasured items, a plant, or flowers, would make a welcome gift.
- ❏ Sing "Weave," by Rosemary Crow, and talk about the power you find in these words.

7. Friendship with God

- ❏ Share memories about best friends from childhood.
- ❏ What traits do you most treasure now in a good friend?
- ❏ Recall the hymn "My God and I," sung by many people during their youth. The words speak of going through fields together, walking, talking, clasping hands, laughing—all as good friends. What meaning did that hymn have for you in the past? What meaning does it hold now?
- ❏ Read together John 15:12-15 where Jesus says, "You are my friends. . . . I have called you friends." Spend time in prayer with your friend who is now a prayer partner.

8. Rejecting God

- ❏ Recall times when you have been criticized or when you have felt rejected by someone you love.
- ❏ When do you think of God as being rejected by your attitudes, your actions? Do you view racist attitudes or actions, carelessness for God's creation, not sharing with others in need as rejection of God?
- ❏ For your worship, use the "Prayer of Confession" (p. 70), followed by the litany "Come, Holy Spirit, Renew the Whole Creation" (p. 72).

9. Doing While Waiting

- ❏ Recall times as a child when you had a hard time waiting for birthdays, for a trip, to go to camp, etc.
- ❏ A familiar poster says "Hurry Up and Wait!" When do you feel this way? How do you wait for spring? What is the best sign of spring for you?

❏ Talk about times of waiting that are difficult: for example, waiting for a medical report, a job offer, approval for a loan, or waiting out a family crisis.

❏ Name some of the scriptures that sustain you during times of waiting. Then bring your concerns about difficult waiting times to God in prayer.

10. The Healing Community

❏ What do you remember from your childhood about being admonished to "tell the truth" or "don't tell a lie?"

❏ Use the video "Is Any Among You Suffering?" that gives personal and congregational stories about anointing for healing. (This video may be ordered from Brethren Press, 1-800-323-8039.)

❏ Talk about ways in which your covenant group has become a healing community for you.

❏ Read the words of the hymn "Anoint Us, Lord" as a prayer (p. 77). Learn the music and sing the hymn as your closing for sharing time.

General Sharing and Prayer Resources

We Are Called

We are called to love and serve others
>To bring good news to the poor, to seek justice, to resist evil;
>To let the oppressed go free, to proclaim Jesus, crucified and risen;
>To proclaim release to the captives, recovery of sight to the blind.

We are called
>To celebrate God's presence, in all the world.
>>By Norm Esdon, from *A New Heart and a New Spirit.*
>>Copyright 1992, Ecumenical Center for Stewardship Studies.
>>Used by permission.

Prayer of Confession

O God, creator of clean hearts and right spirits,
>much of what we do is right—
>>but we do it in the wrong spirit:
>we love our neighbor—
>>for ourselves;
>we do for others—
>>to oblige them to do for us;
>we deny ourselves—
>>to be praised and accepted;
>we seek justice—
>>to get even;
>we resist evil—
>>to further our own cause;
>we love—
>>out of duty;
>we obey—
>>out of fear of punishment
>>or hope of reward;
>we listen to those different from us—
>>with condescending tolerance;
>we exercise dominion over the earth—

as master over slave;
we make peace—
when it suits our purpose;
and we go into the world—
almost all mouth and no ear.

Forgive our wrong-spirited approach, God.
Put a new and right spirit within us.
Fill us with all your fullness.
We ask in the spirit of Christ. Amen.

By Norm Esdon, from *A New Heart and a New Spirit.* Copyright 1992, Ecumenical Center for Stewardship Studies. Used by permission.

Sister Cities

The concern for global awareness in a People of the Covenant group in Modesto, California, led to further study using the book *What About the Russians?* (Brethren Press, 1984). As a result of this study, a group of Modesto people traveled to the Soviet Union, taking with them a peace quilt made by Modesto people as a gift. Eventually Modesto became a sister city to Khmelnitski.

Many US cities have established sister-city relationships. Examples of sister cities (or pending) include:

Alexandria, Virginia .... Kumayri, Armenia
Bloomington/Normal, Illinois.. Vladimir, Russia
Chicago, Illinois .... Kiev, Ukraine
Cincinnati, Ohio .... Kharkiv, Ukraine
Los Angeles, California....... St. Petersburg, Russia
Olympia, Washington .... Samarkand, Uzbekistan
Richmond, Indiana.......... Serpukhov, Russia
Salem, Oregon............. Simferopol, Ukraine
Wenatchee, Washington....... Tynda region, Georgia
Elgin, Illinois.............. Gelgorod, Russia
Lawrence, Kansas .... Lutsk, Ukraine
Tulsa, Oklahoma .... Zelenograd, Russia

To find out whether your town or city has a sister-cities program or to start one, first contact your mayor's office. Then write to Sister Cities International, 120 S. Payne St., Alexandria, VA 22314.

Between the Flood and the Rainbow

This newsletter on environmental teaching and action encourages congregations to "become creation awareness centers, to be actively involved in taking care of the Earth and all of God's Creation." The stewardship of creation is seen as a matter of faith and the environmental crisis as a challenge to Christian faithfulness. The newsletter, edited by Shantilal P. Bhagat, Church of the Brethren staff for Eco-justice and Rural Concerns, is published three times a year. Call 800-323-8039.

A Litany: Come, Holy Spirit, Renew the Whole Creation

Pour out your Holy Spirit, O God,
upon all people of all nations.
Inspire your sons and daughters
to prophesy your gracious love
for all creation.
Fill the young with visions
of justice and peace.
Let the old dream dreams of healing
for your wounded world.

Come, Holy Spirit, renew the whole creation.

Pour out your Holy Spirit, O God,
upon the leaders of the world.
Open their ears to the groans of creation.
Move them with compassion
for the poor and the suffering.
Awaken in them a vision
of a new heaven and a new earth.

Come, Holy Spirit, renew the whole creation.

Pour out your Holy Spirit, O God,
upon your church in every place.
In a world broken by unshared bread,
you call us to offer the body of Christ.
Where blood is spilled
between neighbors and nations,
you invite us to share the blood of Christ.
In a world where hope is fragile,

you wash us with water
for the healing of the nations
and the saving of our souls.
Help us, O God, to be your church,
in spirit and in truth.

Come, Holy Spirit, renew the whole creation.

From 1992 United Nations Conference on
Environment and Development, WCC. Used by permission.

Teach Us To Pray

Lord, sometimes we ought to pray but can't see the need for it.
Sometimes we want to pray but don't know how.
In your own way, in your own time,
    show us how and when and why about prayer,
    just as the Master taught his friends.
Lord, teach us to pray. Amen.

By Ken Gibble. Used by permission.

Anointing Service

The service of anointing for healing, as practiced by the Church of the Brethren, is based on the biblical practice of anointing for healing; James 5:13-16 is a basic text. More information is available in an anointing packet (available from Brethren Press, 1-800-323-8039).

A simple service would include:

• personal indication of need and request for anointing;

• the James 5:13-16 text;

• brief words about God's will for wholeness in body, mind, spirit;

• an opportunity for confession, for seeking peace with God;

• an assurance of pardon;

• brief words spoken during the anointing, such as:

Upon your confession of faith and your willingness to commit your life to God, you are anointed with oil for the forgiveness of sin, for the strengthening of faith, and for healing and wholeness according to God's grace and wisdom.

- a few drops of oil are placed on the finger(s), touched to the person's forehead three times, once as each purpose is stated;

- hands are lightly placed on the person's head, and prayers offered.

My Life Flows On

Robert Lowry, 1869, alt.   Robert Lowry, 1869

1. My life flows on in end - less song, a - bove earth's lam - en - ta - tion I
2. Through all the tu - mult and the strife, I hear that mu - sic ring - ing. It
3. What though my joys and com - forts die? The Lord my Sav - ior liv - eth. What
4. The peace of Christ makes fresh my heart, a foun - tain ev - er spring - ing! All

catch the sweet, though far off hymn that hails a new cre - a - tion.
finds an ech - o in my soul. How can I keep from sing - ing?
though the dark - ness ga - ther round? Songs in the night he giv - eth.
things are mine since I am his! How can I keep from sing - ing?

REFRAIN

No storm can shake my in - most calm while to that Rock I'm cling - ing. Since

love is Lord of heav'n and earth, how can I keep from sing - ing?

Brothers and Sisters of Mine

Kenneth I. Morse, 1974

Wilbur E. Brumbaugh, 1974

1. Broth - ers and sis - ters of mine are the hun - gry who sigh in their
2. Strang - ers and neigh - bors, they claim my at - ten - tion; they sleep by my
3. Peo - ple are they, men and wom - en and chil - dren, and each has a
4. Lord of all liv - ing, we make our con - fess - ion: Too long we have

sor - row and weep in their pain. Sis - ters and broth - ers of mine are the
door - step, they sit by my bed. Neigh - bors and strang - ers, their an - guish con-
heart keep-ing time with my own. Peo - ple are they, per - sons made in God's
wast - ed the wealth of our lands. Lord of all lov - ing, re - new our com-

home - less who wait with - out shel - ter from wind and from rain.
cerns me, and I must not feast till the hun - gry are fed.
im - age, so what shall I of - fer them, bread or a stone?
pass - ion and o - pen our hearts while we reach out our hands.

Anoint Us, Lord

John David Bowman   John David Bowman

1. A - noint us, Lord, we feel the need ____ of your strength; Flow through our lives ____ with your love. ____ Pour your cool - ing oils ___ down, give us sound - ness of breath. Bring your Spir - it like a dove.

2. A - noint us, Lord, we are sick ____ and a - lone; Lone - ly and lost we seek re - lief. ____ Pour your cool - ing oils ___ down, while ____ prayers of faith we raise. New ____ life we shall re - ceive.

3. A - noint us, Lord, we want to give our - selves to you, Strengths ____ and weak - ness - es a - like. ____ Pour your cool - ing oils ___ down, and ____ con - se - crate our lives. We ____ give our - selves to you.

4. A - noint us, Lord, we feel the need ____ of your strength; Flow through our lives ____ with your love. ____ Pour your cool - ing oils ___ down, give us sound - ness of breath. Bring your Spir - it like a dove.

Other Covenant Bible Studies available from *faithQuest*: